First Position Scale Studies

for

the Cello
book one
by Cassia Harvey

Contents

C Major: First Octave	2
G Major: First Octave	6
D Major: Second Octave	10
F Major: First Octave	14
C Major: Second Octave	18
E-Flat Major: First Octave	22
B-Flat Major: First Octave	26
D Major: First Octave	30
A Major: First Octave	34
Scales to Play With Vibrato	38
Fast Scale Studies	42
Major Scales in First Position With Non-Traditional Fingerings	48
Some Major Arpeggios in First Position	51

CHP179

©2011 by C. Harvey Publications All Rights Reserved.

www.charveypublications.com - print books
www.learnstrings.com - PDF downloadable books
www.harveystringarrangements.com - chamber music

C Major: First Octave

Cassia Harvey

Slurs

Scale Rhythms

©2011 C. Harvey Publications All Rights Reserved.

Dotted Quarter Note Rhythms

G Major: First Octave

First Position Scale Studies for the Cello, Book One

Slurs

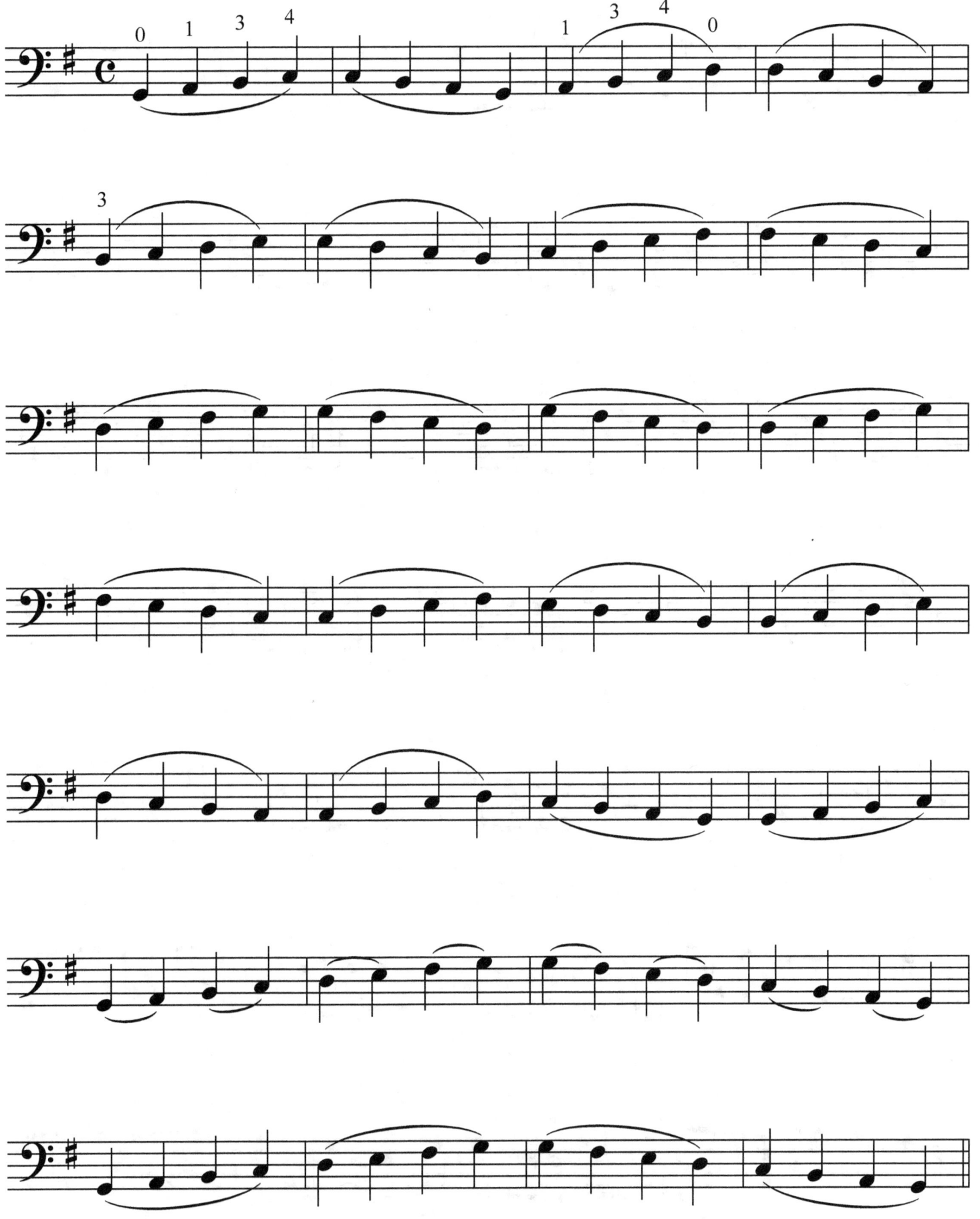

Scale Rhythms

6/8 Timing

D Major: First Octave

First Position Scale Studies for the Cello, Book One

Slurs

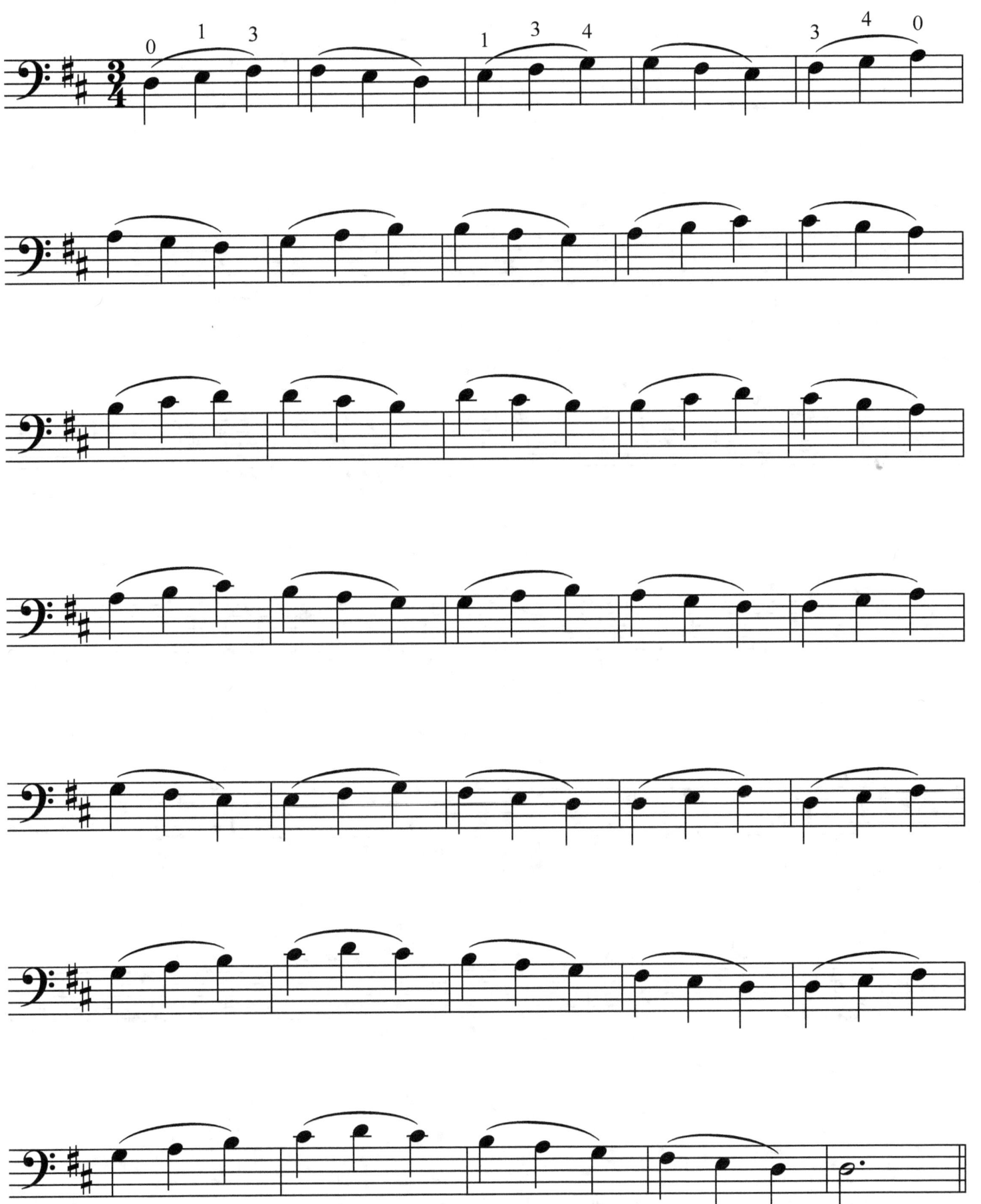

©2011 C. Harvey Publications All Rights Reserved.

Scale Rhythms

First Position Scale Studies for the Cello, Book One

Trills

©2011 C. Harvey Publications All Rights Reserved.

F Major: First Octave

Slurs

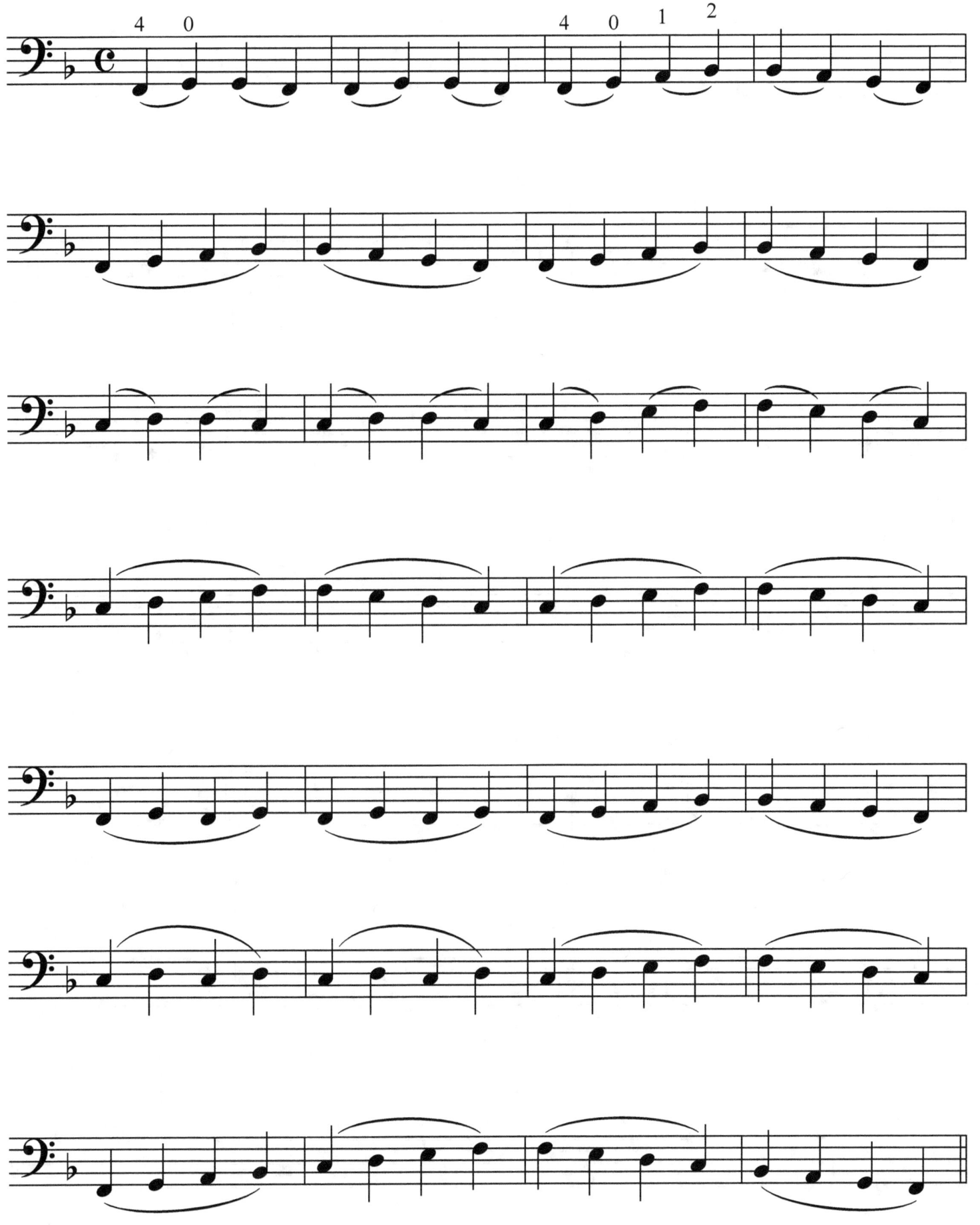

Dotted Quarter Note Rhythms

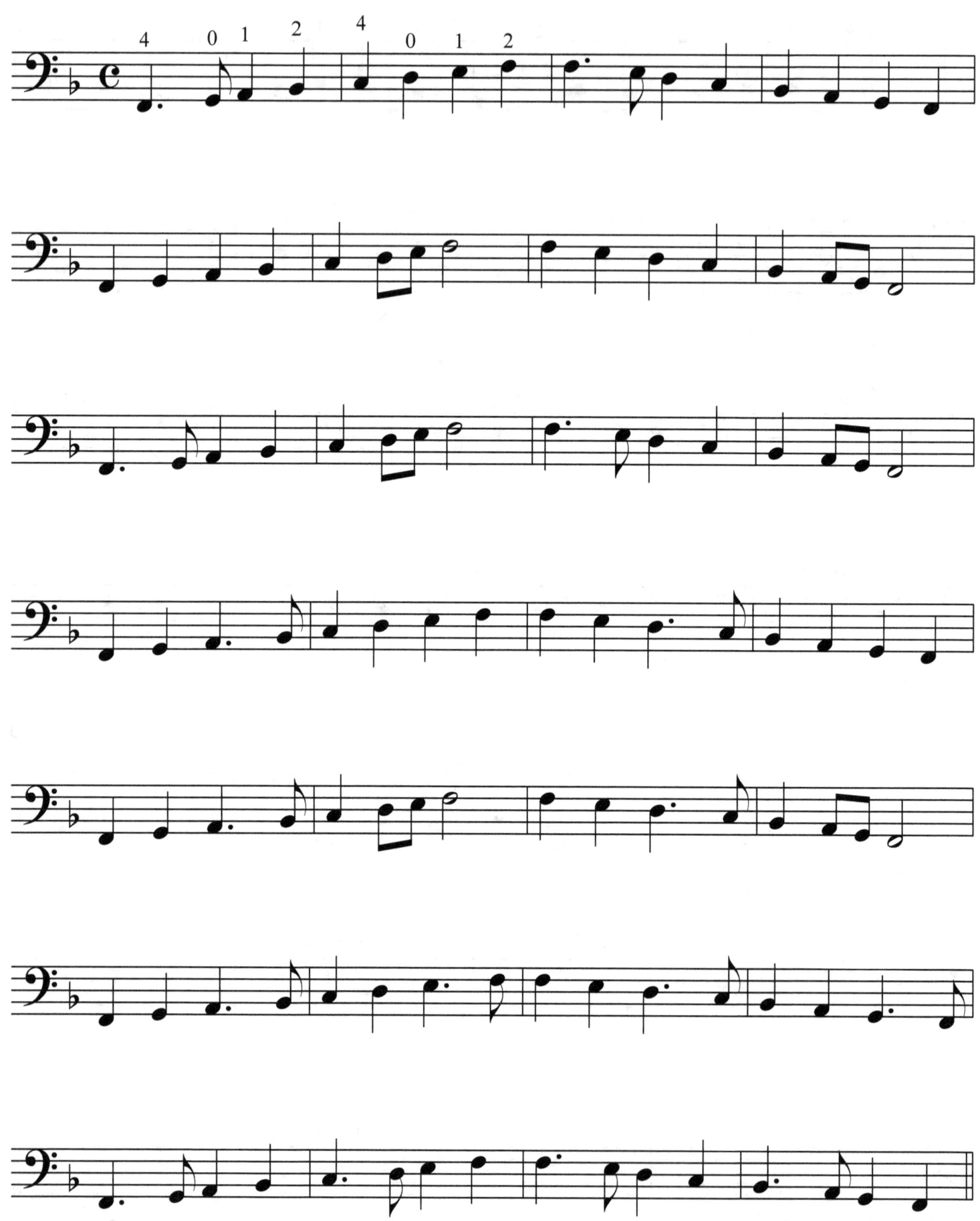

6/8 Timing

C Major: Second Octave

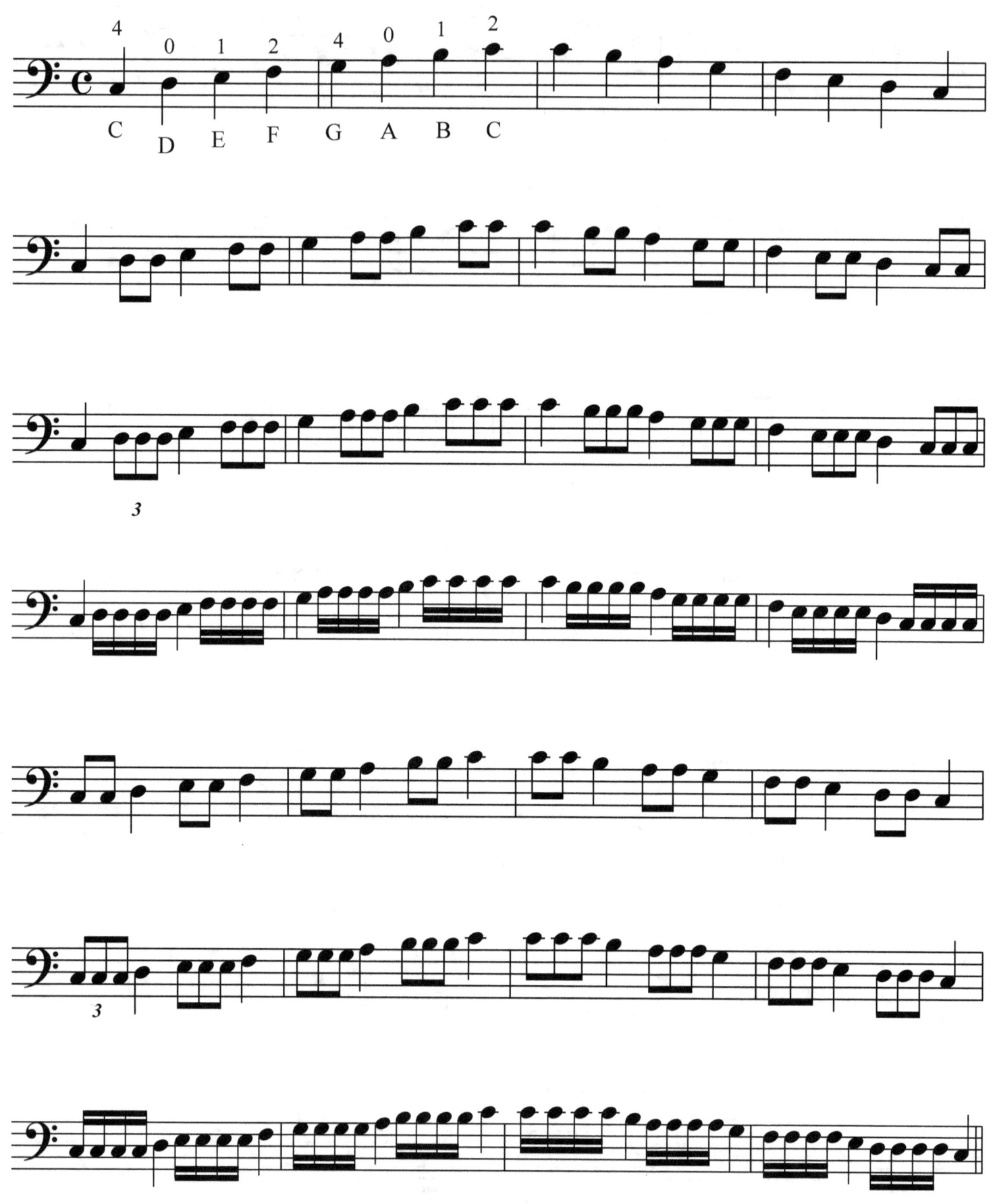

Slurs

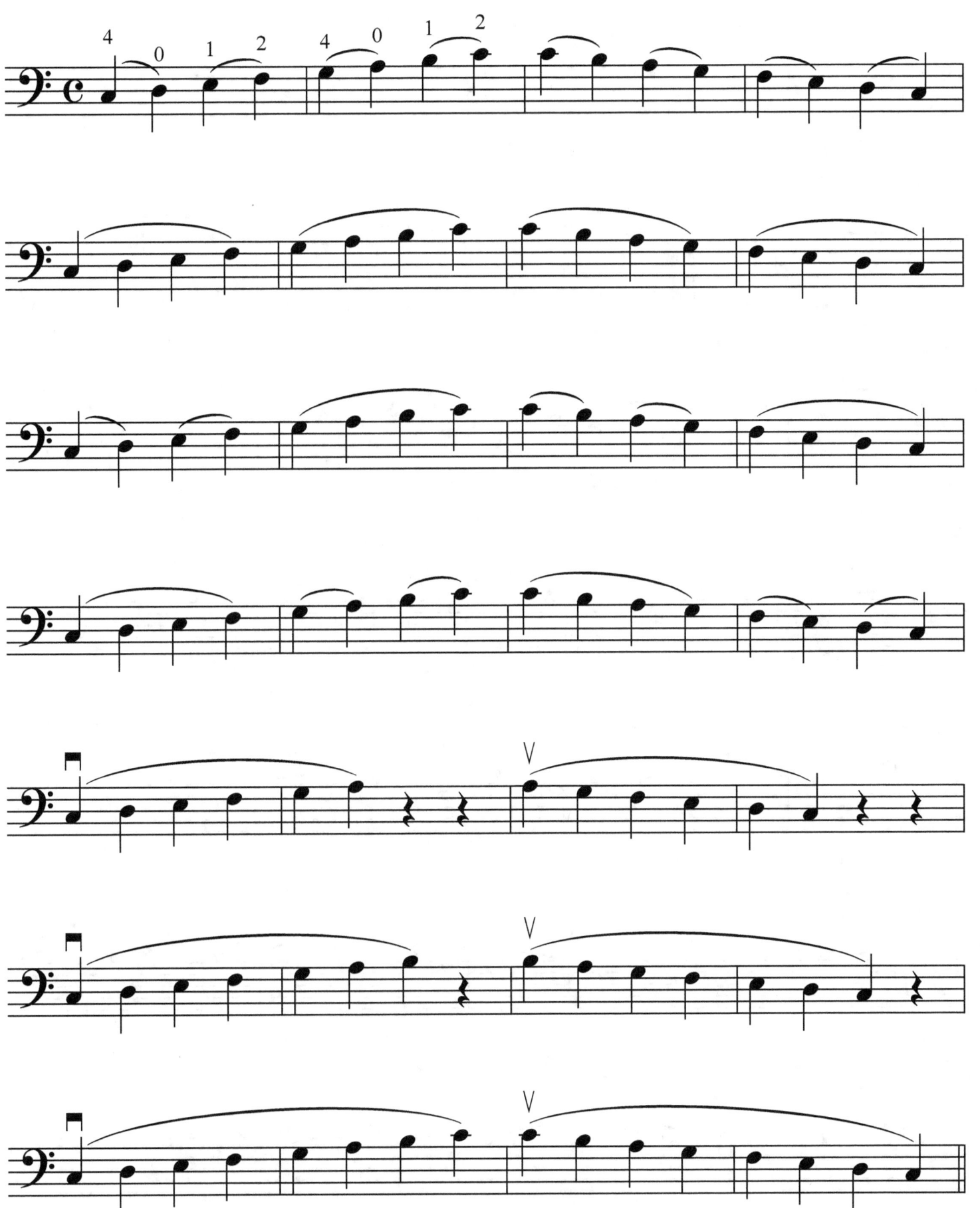

Dotted Quarter Note Rhythms

6/8 Timing

E♭ Major: First Octave

First Position Scale Studies for the Cello, Book One

Scale Rhythms

Slurs

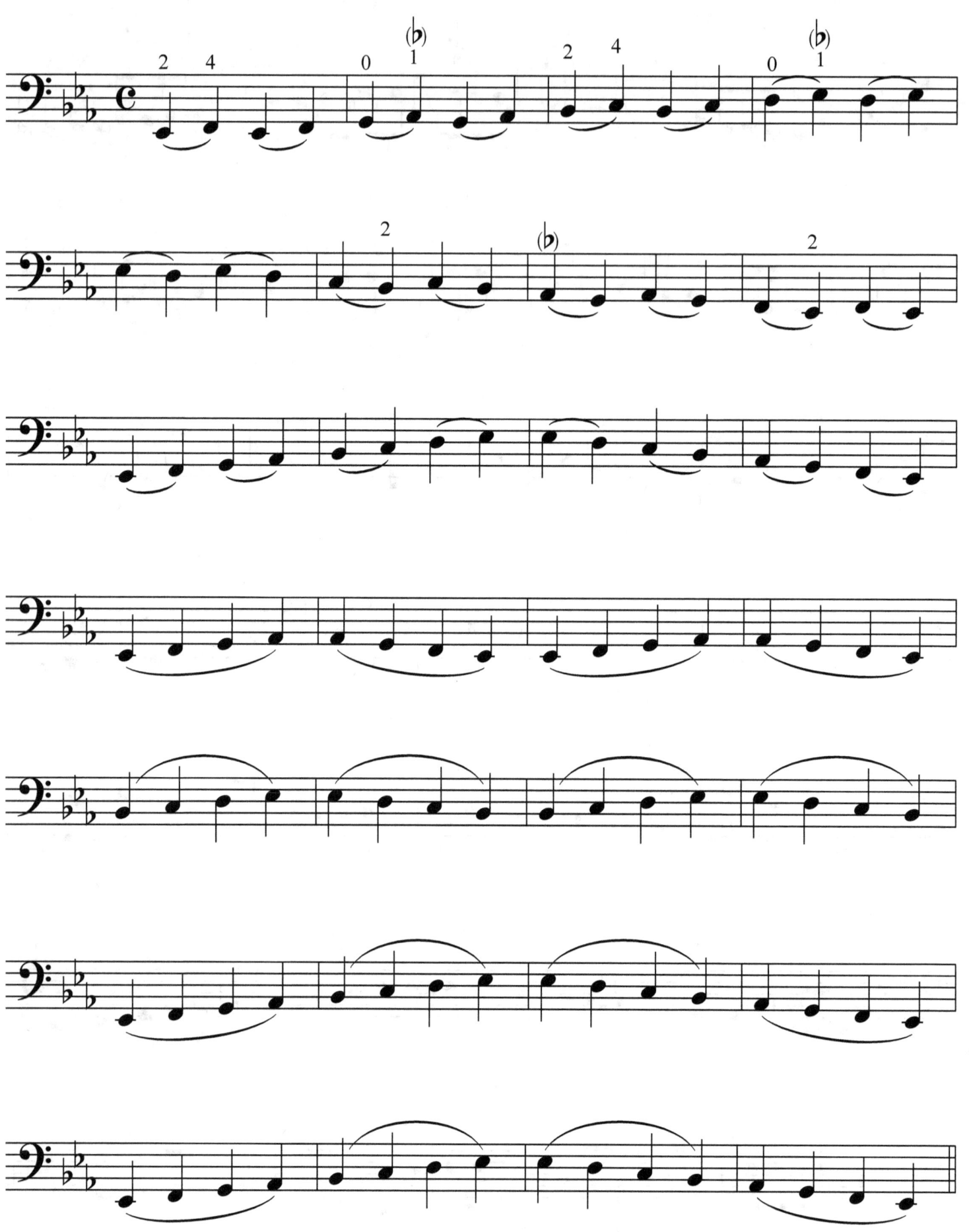

First Position Scale Studies for the Cello, Book One

Scale Finger Workout

©2011 C. Harvey Publications All Rights Reserved.

B♭ Major: First Octave

First Position Scale Studies for the Cello, Book One

Slurs

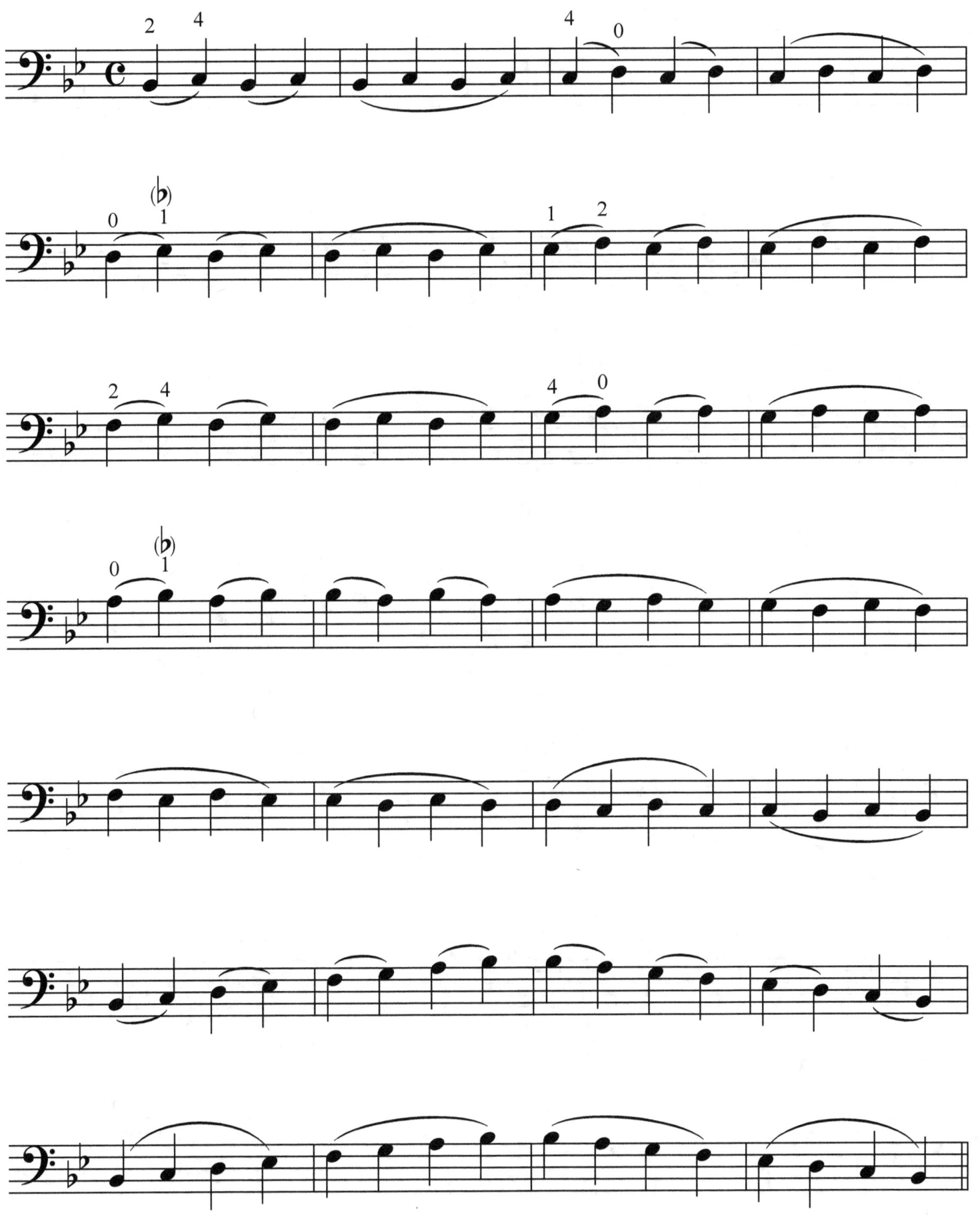

©2011 C. Harvey Publications All Rights Reserved.

Dotted Quarter Note Rhythms

First Position Scale Studies for the Cello, Book One

3/4 Timing

D Major: First Octave

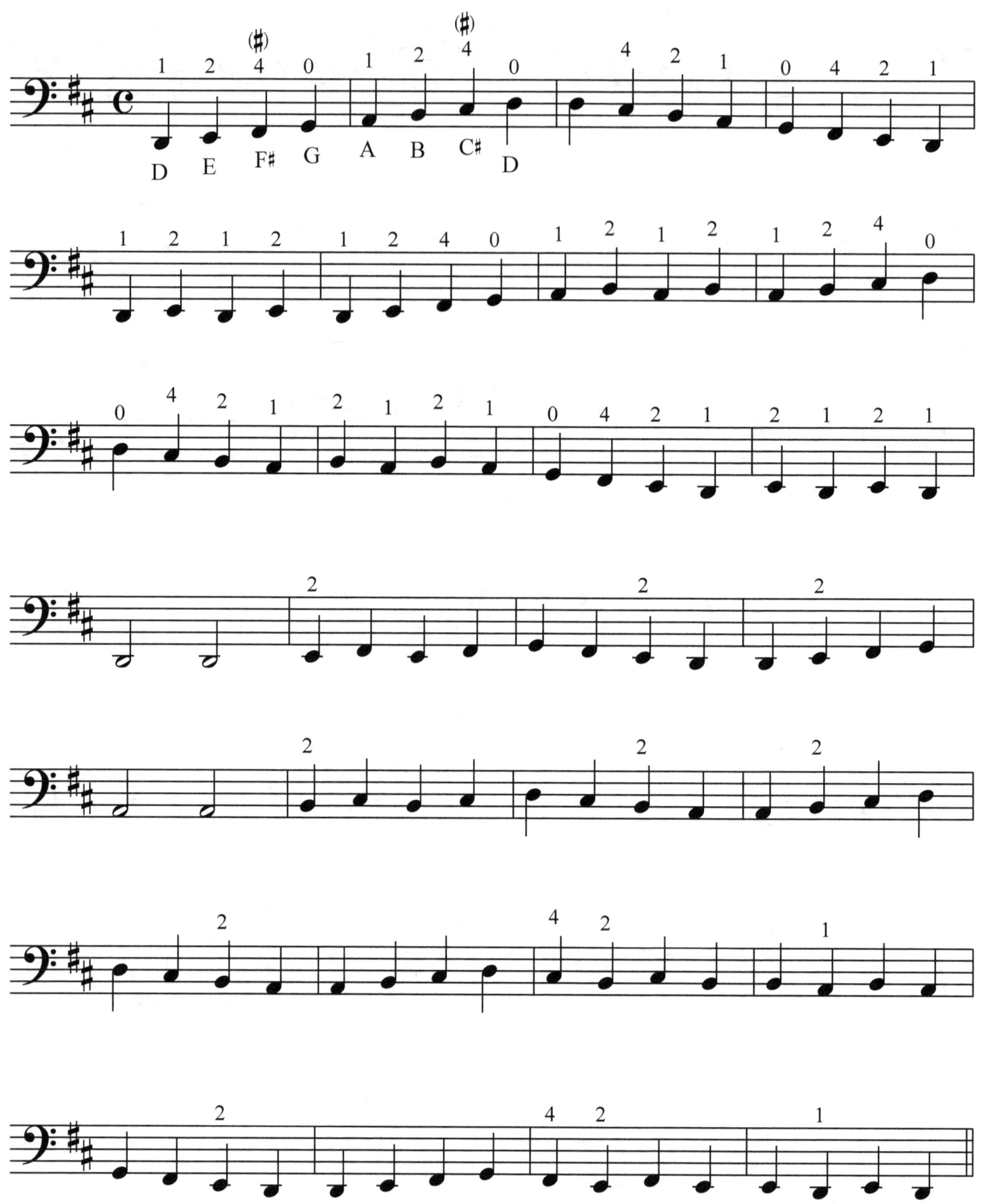

First Position Scale Studies for the Cello, Book One

Slurs

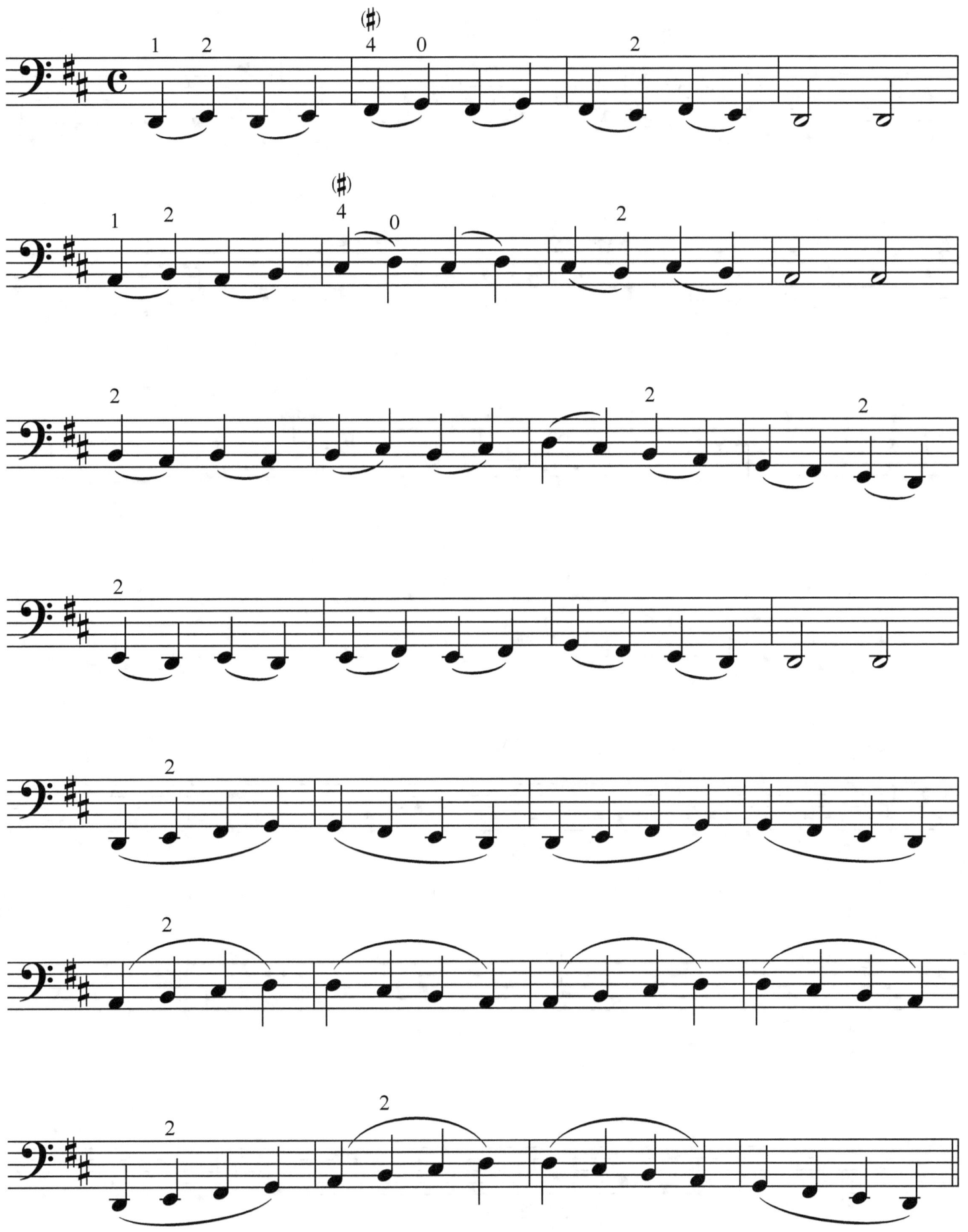

©2011 C. Harvey Publications All Rights Reserved.

Scale Rhythms

Slurs in 3/4 Timing

A Major: First Octave

First Position Scale Studies for the Cello, Book One

Slurs

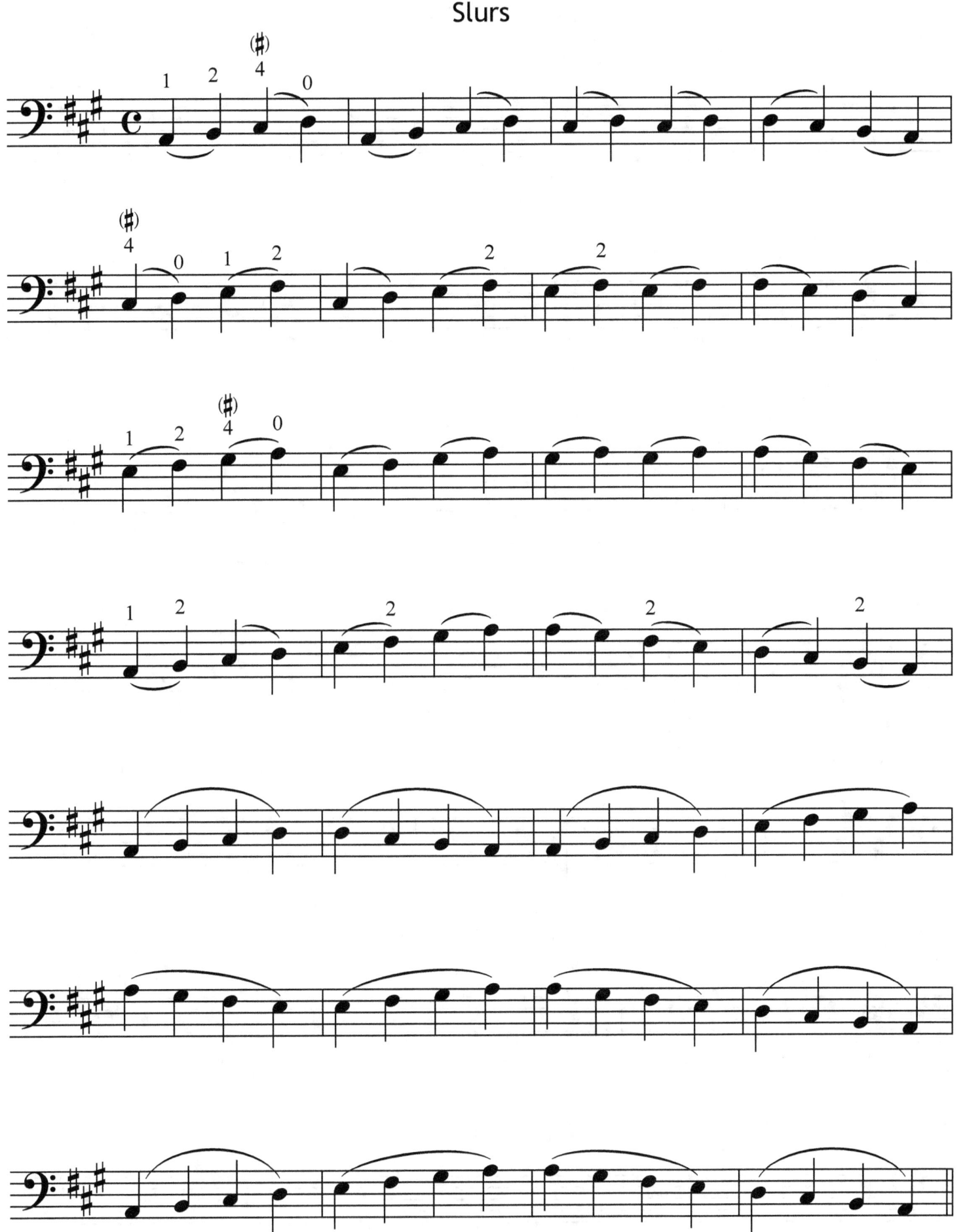

Scale Rhythms

6/8 Timing

Scales to play with Vibrato

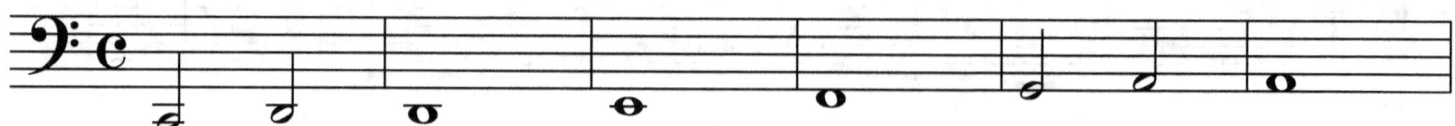

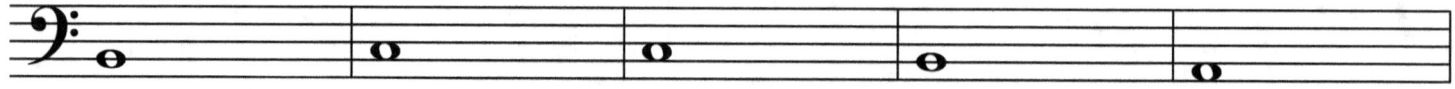

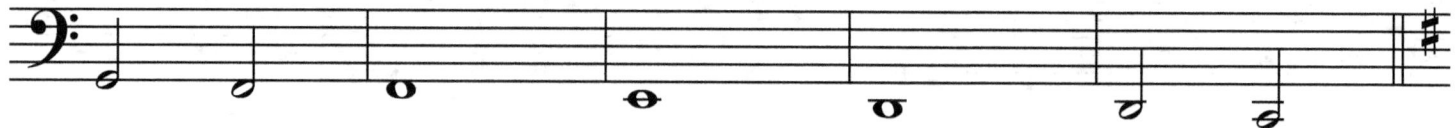

First Position Scale Studies for the Cello, Book One

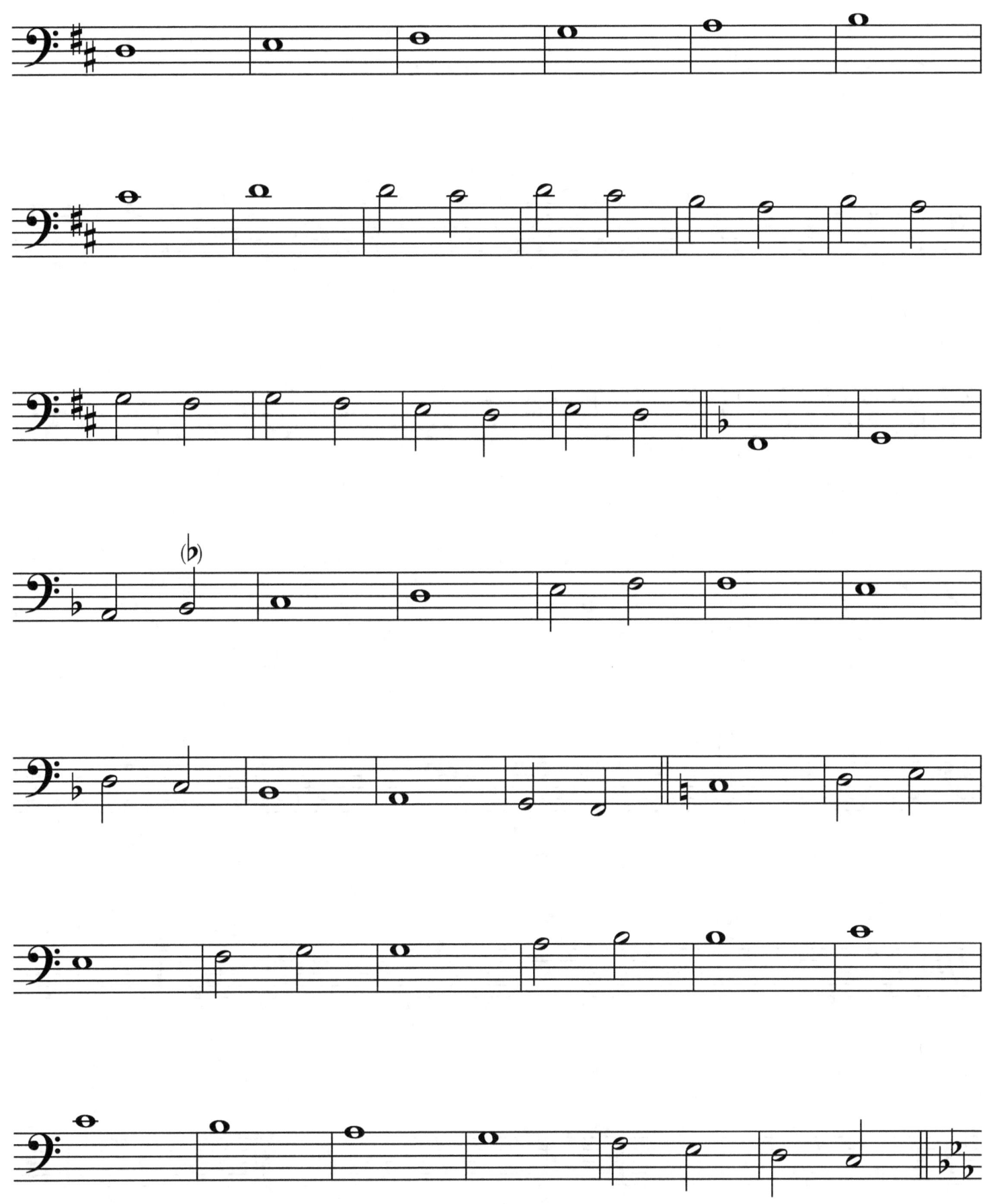

First Position Scale Studies for the Cello, Book One

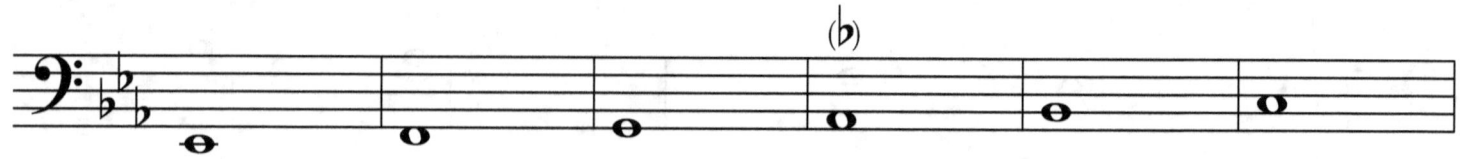

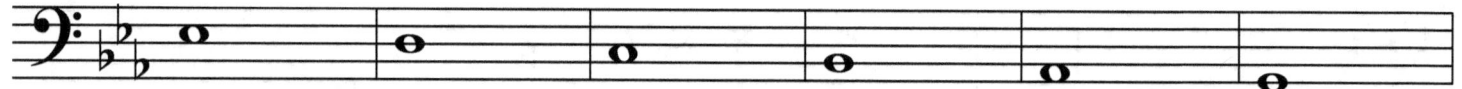
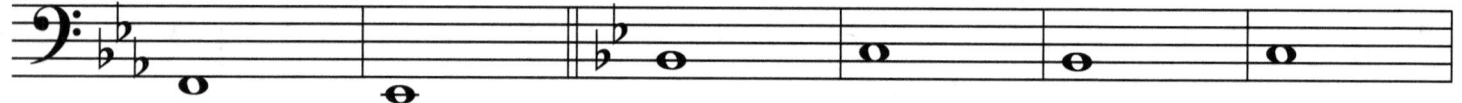
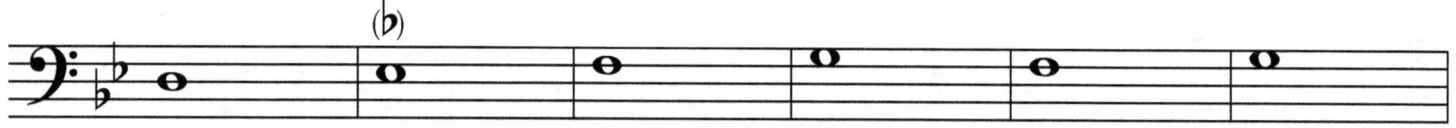
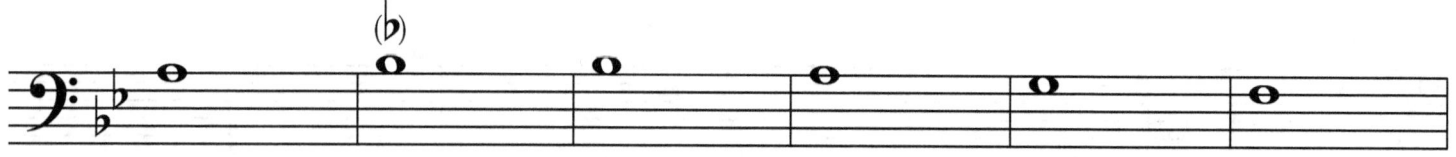

©2011 C. Harvey Publications All Rights Reserved.

First Position Scale Studies for the Cello, Book One

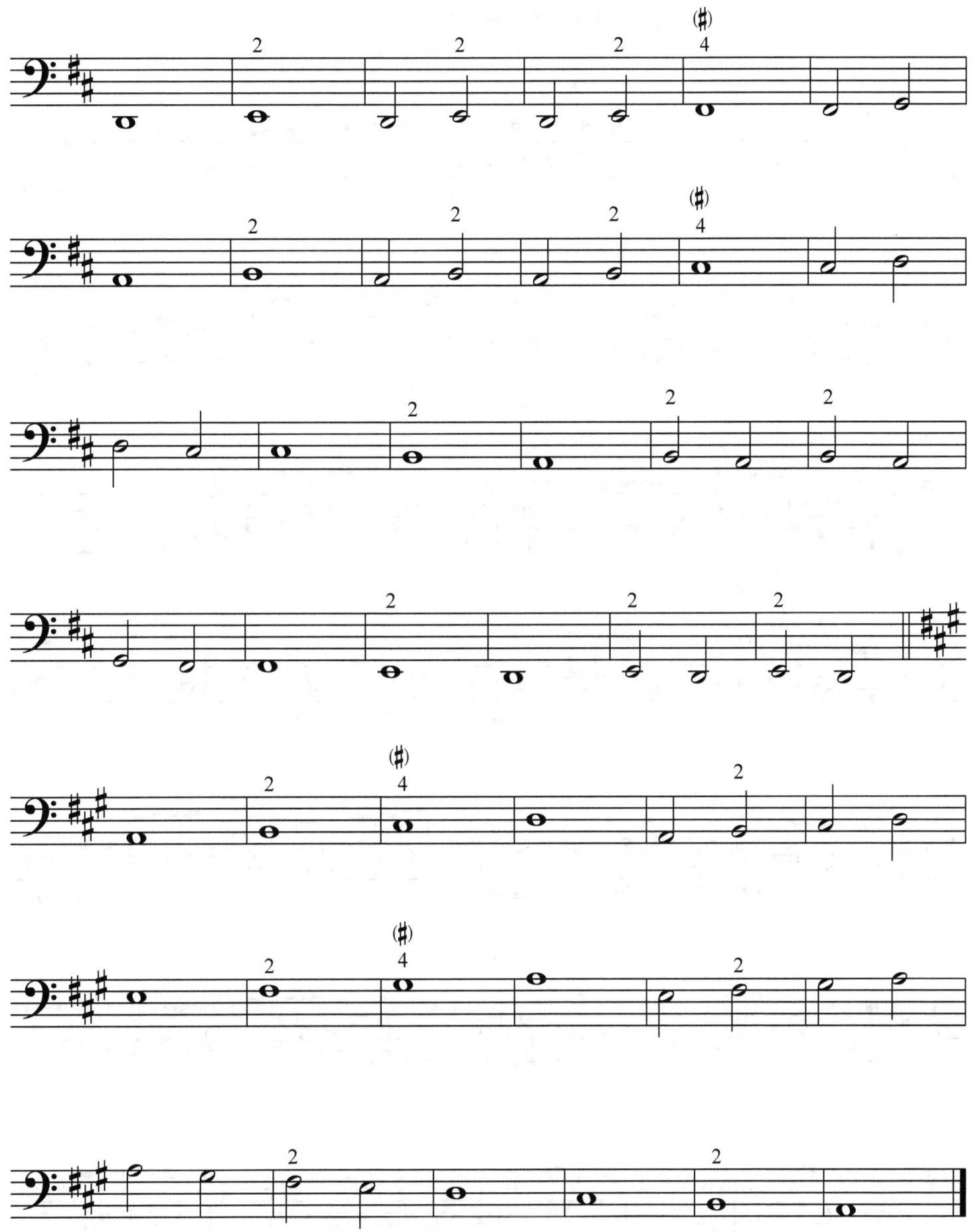

Fast Scale Studies

First Position Scale Studies for the Cello, Book One

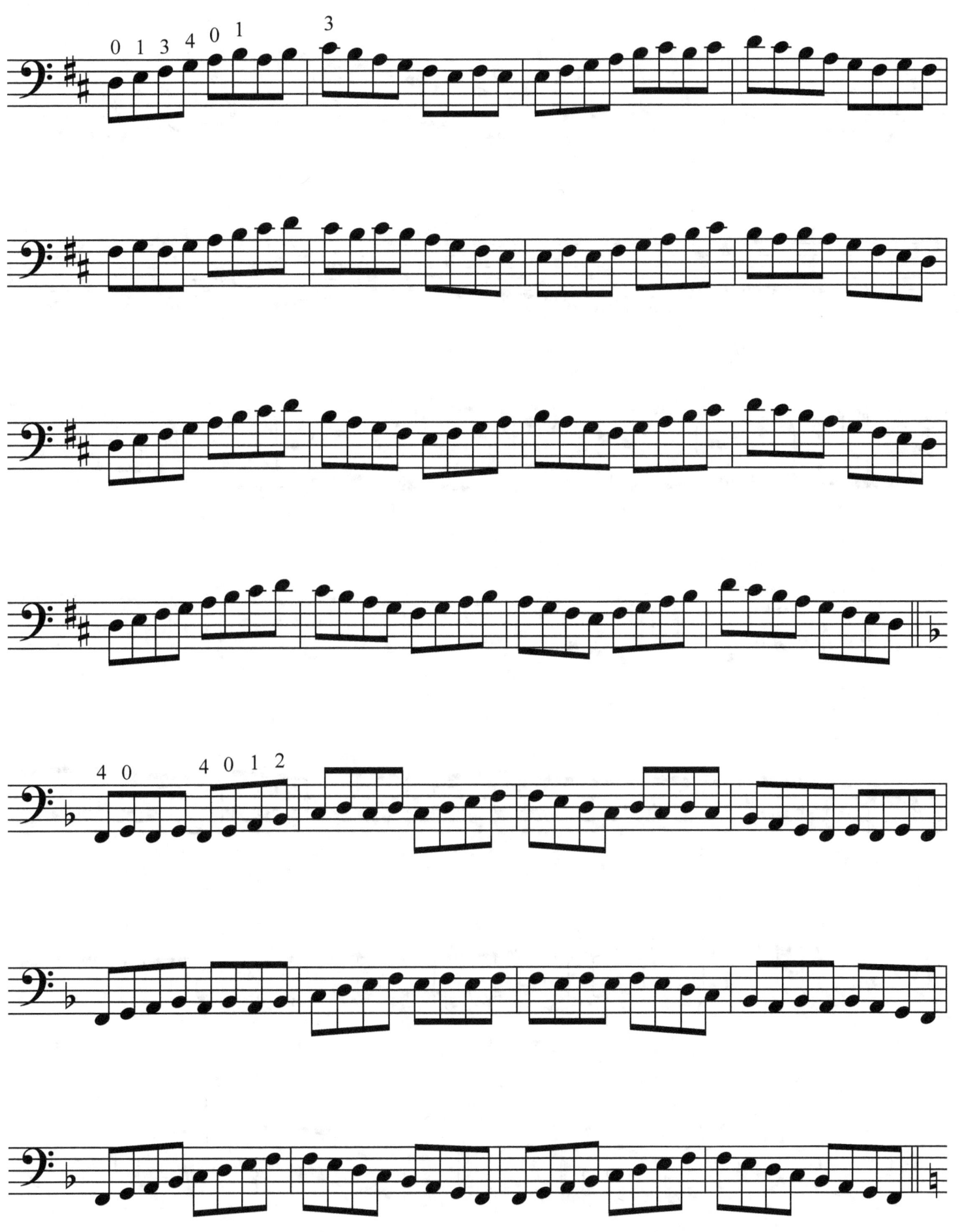

44 First Position Scale Studies for the Cello, Book One

First Position Scale Studies for the Cello, Book One

46 First Position Scale Studies for the Cello, Book One

First Position Scale Studies for the Cello, Book One

All Major Scales in First Position With Some Non-Traditional Fingerings

Note: Many of the next scales typically use fingerings that shift out of first position. These traditional fingerings are found in *The Two Octaves Book for Cello (CHP122)*, *Learning Three-Octave Scales on the Cello (CHP356)*, and *Three-Octave Scales for Cello, Book One (CHP152)*.

The scales below do not use those traditional fingerings. Instead, they are included to give cellists an idea of all of the notes that can be reached from first position using extensions.

I = A String
II = D String
III = G String
IV = C String

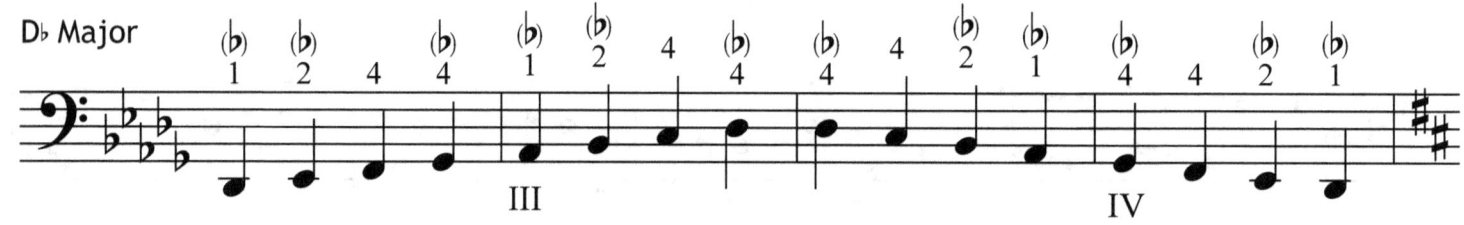

©2011 C. Harvey Publications All Rights Reserved.

First Position Scale Studies for the Cello, Book One

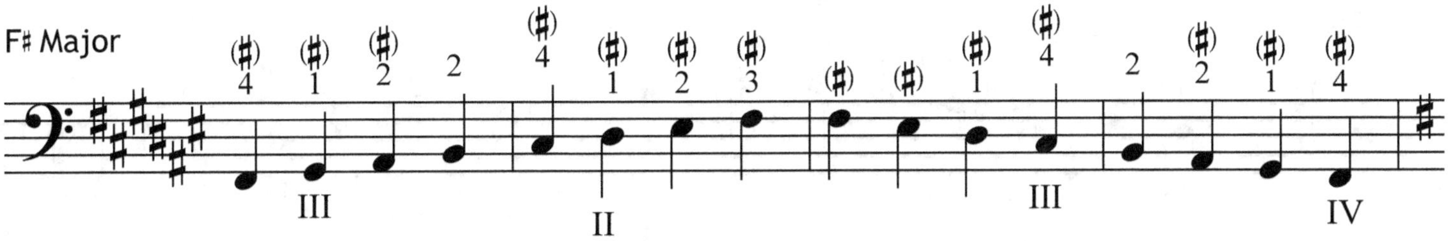

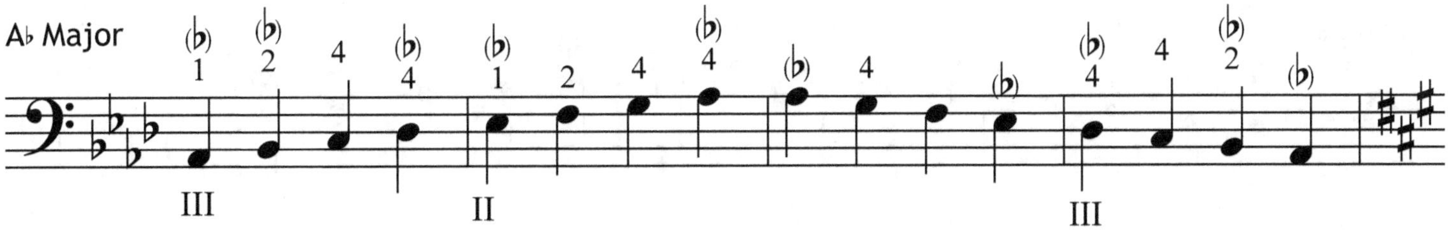

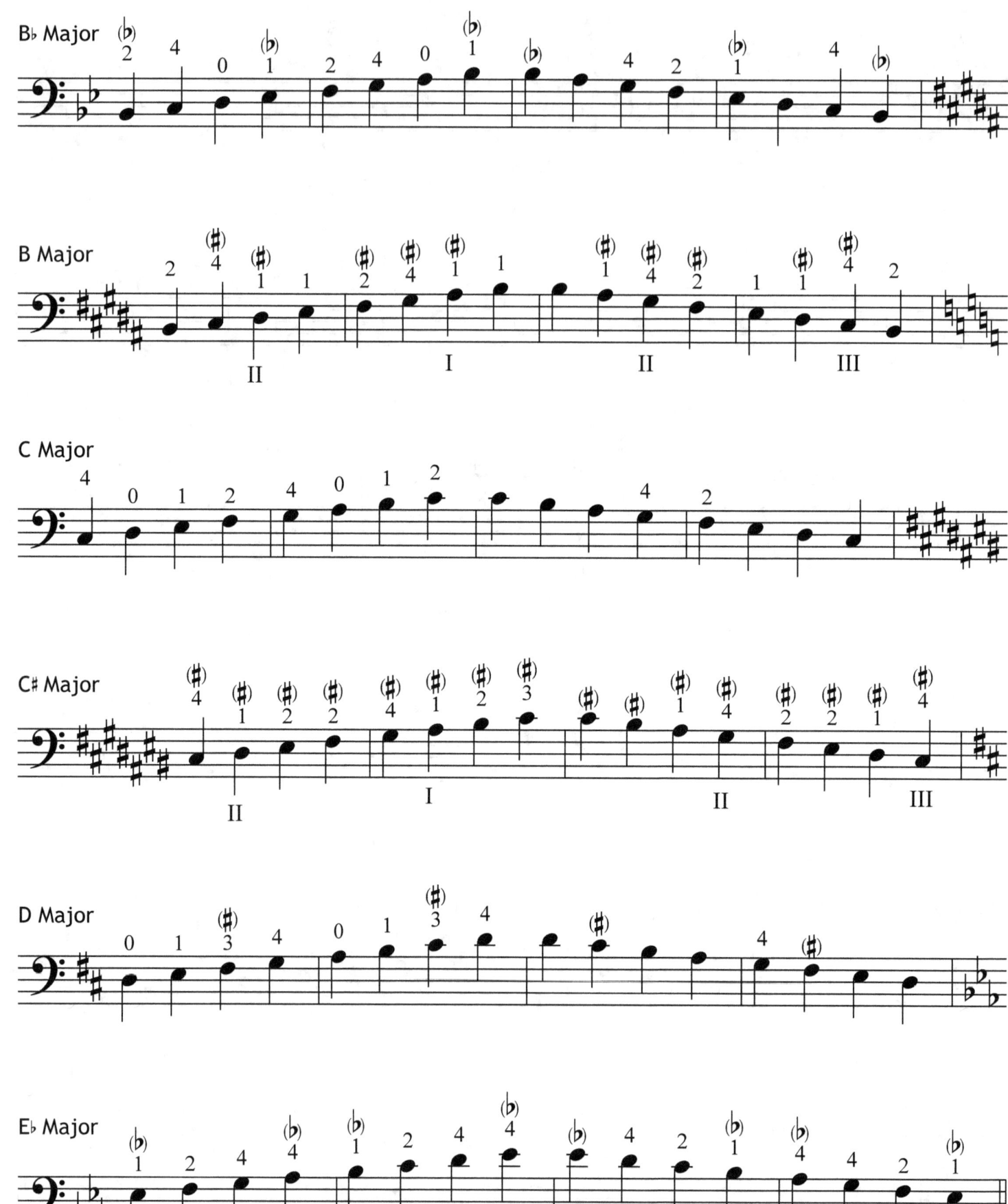

Some Major Arpeggios in First Position

www.ingramcontent.com/pod-product-compliance
Lightning Source LLC
Chambersburg PA
CBHW051425070526
44584CB00023B/3580